Best of British

a celebration of inspirational floristry

edited & compiled by
Liz Cowling NDSF FSF

For those people who share our dreams...

"Whether you can do, or dream you can, begin it.
Boldness has genius, power and magic in it."

Goethe

First published in 2002 by Billet doux Design co.
Orchard House, Coney Weston, Bury St Edmunds, Suffolk IP31 1HG Telephone 01359 221421

Text & concept © 2002 Elizabeth Cowling NDSF FSF

Floristry: Various contributors from around the British Isles
Photography: Various contributors from around the British Isles - see individual acknowledgements
Sketches: Lizzie Jackson, Bury St Edmunds, Telephone 01284 701406
Design layout: Liz and Ben Cowling together with Colin Barber, Old Newton Graphics, Suffolk. Telephone 01449 675548
Print: Reflex Litho, Thetford, Norfolk. Telephone 01842 754600

A catalogue record for this book is available from the British Library.
ISBN No: 0-9541960-2-3

Best of British

a celebration of inspirational floristry

A thing of beauty is a joy for ever,
It's loveliness increases; it will never
Pass into nothingness; but still will keep
A bower quiet for us, and a sleep
Full of sweet dreams, and health,
              and quiet breathing...

John Keates

foreword by
Angela Turner NDSF FSF
President, Society of Floristry Ltd

When embarking upon a career in floristry little did I realise that it would become not only a wonderful addiction, but a way of life.

Working with natural materials presents endless design possibilities. A constantly open and enquiring mind allows you to enjoy a passionate affair with plant material. Embrace their spirit and character, let them entwine your soul. wonder at their beauty.

Working on the emotional front line requires a floral designer to be multifaceted; professional and skilled in many areas. Floristry is fast becoming a recognised art form. Creating an image. Inspiring a lifestyle. All of this requires dedication and commitment to our craft.

The Society of Floristry was founded in the UK in 1951 with the sole purpose of raising and upholding the standards in floristry world-wide. The National Diploma of the Society of Floristry is the highest qualification for professional floristry in Great Britain.

The majority of the contributors to this book, as well as the Editor, have achieved this and still they constantly strive to produce work to the highest possible degree of artistic innovation and perfection.

This compilation of work by some of Britain's most innovative florists is living proof that the work of the founder members of the Society of Floristry is being carried on today.

The Best of British - a celebration of inspirational floristry. Dedicated professionals... pure artists...

INTRODUCTION

Floristry and flower arranging are subjects that can be as simple and casual or as detailed and sophisticated as either the mood or occasion demands. They are also subjects that touch all nationalities and ages - young and not so young, men, women and children - for happy and sad occasions, and everyday...

Nature provides us with a seemingly never ending supply of materials in a vast range of form, texture, size and colour. Each and every one of us sees that material in a different light, and in a different way. There are numerous books celebrating the skills of 'flower arrangers' but rarely by the people who professionally help us to celebrate, remember or simply 'say it with flowers.' All the contributors share the same passion and love for their subject and all have an abiding love and respect for nature coupled with an insatiable appetite to learn more and a strong desire to share their knowledge and skills. Their work is varied, reflecting their own personalities, preferences and styles. They come from all all across these glorious islands - including Eire... From their scanty brief just a few months ago some wonderful examples of floristry have evolved. The work that they have created shows a glimpse of what British florists do every day. It is a celebration, it is inspirational and it is by some of the "best.' Enjoy!

Liz Cowling NDSF FSF, 2002

Coral Carter NDSF AIFD FSF

Coral is one of those florists who has amassed such a broad knowledge of the industry over the years, but still loves to learn new techniques and share her skills, enthusiasm and love for flowers with everyone. Born into a horticultural nursery background, it seems that Coral was destined to become a florist. She was actually taking on the family business at the tender age of 12 due to her mother's retirement, and since she has been with the industry, Coral's work has taken her all over the world and has resulted in many accolades throughout the industry. Coral has won numerous Chelsea gold medals for her displays. She is a former International FTD Interflora Cup Champion in 1996 and 1997, and won such numerous other prestigious competitions as well as being presented with the Interflora Bill Evans Award for services to the industry.

"Take the Society of Floristry's examinations, attend as many training courses and events as possible. Compete if at all possible, It is the greatest learning curve there is. All these factors and experiences will ensure that you develop your own unique style."

Claire Cowling ICSF MSF

Claire is a young florist who likes nothing better than to be engrossed in some floral design that involves intricate detail. She is always on the look-out for new and innovative ways to use materials, while using the utmost respect for those materials. During the years that she has been in the business she has been awarded many prizes for professional floristry at national shows, as well as designing pieces for a Gold medal winning entry of professional floristry at Chelsea Flower Show. In her quest for gaining knowledge Claire has also participated in many workshops and demonstrations by International desigers, as well as travelling and working in Finland. Over the past few months she has been studying for her teaching certificate, and creating designs for other floristry titles co-written by her mother and herself, inbetween marketing the books and planning a series of workshops for various subject areas.

"It is vitally important to learn the basics thoroughly first, and cultivate a good deal of 'patience' to enable detailed work to be carried out well."

Karen Lamb NDSF AIFD FSF

Karen is a well-known British florist who has made her mark on the world circuit as well as nearer to home... She runs a floristry business in Yorkshire, demonstrates floristry both in this country and U.S.A. and participates in professional competitions, including the Chelsea Flower Show, where she has attained a Silver Gilt medal for professional floristry. Always on the look-out for new inspiration and ideas, Karen understands how important it is to continue learning, be it from other designers, the media, the fashion industry or, most important, nature. She is particularly interested in the Scandinavian style and loves to work with rich, vibrant colours and most especially clashing colours.

"Be artistic, and prepared to work long and hard for little financial reward, be positive, motivated and focused on what you want to achieve - and go for it! The self satisfaction of creating designs with wonderful materials is great."

Mike Shapcott

Mike is one of those rare people who has a true affinity to nature and a genuine love of all natural materials, but most especially foliage - of any kind. This is reflected in his designs which focus heavily on the use of many and varied kinds of garden foliage wherever possible. All inspiration comes directly from Mother Nature and the glorious gifts that are available for use. Mike has worked in many countries - both exhibitions and demonstrations and thoroughly enjoys competing. Over the years Mike has achieved many notable successes at the Chelsea flower show - winning all the range of medals - including the coveted Gold, as well as the Tudor Rose at the Hampton Court flower show. He is based in Hampshire where he works, and in his spare time, enjoys breeding, showing and judging Chihuahuas.

"Look, learn and listen... Keep an open mind about every design you see, don't have tunnel vision. I believe the greatest way to pass my passion on is by demonstrating my skills..."

Nina Sherson NZPFA AIFD NDSF FSF

Nina's career in floristry has taken her all over the world, and she has an insatiable appetite for exploring new ideas, techniques and concepts. Since opening her business in the West End of London in 1990 she has continued to develop her eclectic style of design. She has won the prestigious Interflora Florist of the year competition – winning all eight categories – something that had never been achieved before, as well as numerous Chelsea flower show medals for professional floristry, including the coveted Gold and 'Best in Show' 2000.   Nina understands the need to 'give back' to the industry that she loves. Together with her partner Franck she gives freely of her time. As late as 1996 they were together instructing, running their own business, and demonstrating across the world. A designer of extraordinary insight Nina is able to weave the elements of reality and imagination into human led design.

"My motivation in design is to bring the consumer and the industry into focus, and to go back to the preservation of nature. The importance of stewardship and conservation of natural, constructed and human resources is vital."

Margaret Stewart NDSF FSF

Throughout her long professional career in floristry Margaret has believed passionately in the wisdom of sharing and passing on her wealth of knowledge. She has received many accolades during those years, competed very successfully - winning two coveted Gold medals for professional floristry, four times Scottish Florist of the year, as well as Interflora Designer of the Year for Great Britain and World Cup Assistant Designer. She has been a floristry tutor and demonstrator both nationally and internationally, as well as running a demanding and successful retail business in Glasgow. And still, the passion is there...

"In this fast changing world we live in, floristry has to be completely professional to survive, we must offer a service second to none, only then will we still be there, amongst the craftsmen of the world."

Neil Whittaker NDSF AIFD FSF

Neil loves to push forward the boundaries of floral design and floristry techniques - to be able to understand why, where and how plant material grows, to understand better their characteristics, their natural form, and how to show them at their best. He does this from his business base in Manchester, as well as by travelling and participating in events and competitions throughout the world. He has been UK Teleflorist of the year which led to him becoming 1st runner up in the Teleflorist World Cup. Neil enjoys passing on his knowledge through workshops and demonstrations, and intends hosting more Master Classes for forward thinking florists at his purpose built design studio. He is never happier than when he is designing and promoting floristry, whether it's traditional, or contemporary, in British or European style.

"I believe it is vitally important to open the mind, to see things in a new light and push forward the boundaries of design. A willingness to share concepts and understanding allows our designs and techniques to evolve."

Jim Williamson NDSF FSF

Jim is the third generation in the family business, established in 1935, with an awesome total of eleven shops, a central make-up unit, a garden centre and sixty seven staff. Jim still has the ability to 'wow' with his inspirational floristry even though much of his time is now spent in business administration as opposed to hands-on floristry. Over the years he has amassed an enviable collection of accolades including UK & Scottish Interflora Florist of the Year, a much coveted Gold medal for professional floristry at the Chelsea Flower Show, and has represented the UK in the floristry World Cup twice, achieving 6th and 7th places respectively. Jim favours structured, non fussy designs in vibrant colours.. He is married with a young son and lives in the picturesque Scottish countryside.

"Our trade is not life from a way, it is a way of life. If you are prepared to put in your life it will give you back only satisfaction. Be prepared to put something in and you will get something out. Always look and learn, never accepting that you have learnt enough."

Vinny Yeates AIFD

Vinny is an enthusiastic young designer who has been employed in the family business since leaving school some seven years ago. Winning a competition in 1995 whetted his appetite for extending his design skills and broadening his horizons. In 1998 he represented Ireland at the Eurofleurs competition. The millennium proved to be another exciting year as Vinny designed a stand for the prestigious Chelsea Flower Show professional floristry competitions and was delighted to be awarded a Silver Gilt medal for his interpretation of the theme. Although still only in his twenties Vinny is proving that he intends to really make his mark on the professional floristry scene. He has recently completed his AIFD portfolio, and is furthering his career working on corporate functions and events in New York to get an even broader picture.

"With energy, an open mind and bags of enthusiasm anything is achievable."

ENTANGLEMENT

a stunning bouquet full of movement and sentiment. Long slender stems of Cornus bound tightly and formed into a lazy ring with a long, sweeping tail makes the initial statement. Soft, downy Platycerium leaves add a dramatic flourish to the overall shape, which has long trails of Rhipsalis and Columnea domestica. Carefully placed Phalaenopsis orchids add a touch of luxury and wonderful contrast to the near black Zantedeshia and stunning Hellebores clustered near the focal area.

... imagine a perfect morning, warm Caribbean sea, clear blue skies, and the anticipation of a new life together. This innovative, free-moving bridal bouquet captures the essence of a day filled with emotion in an exotic island location. The segmented Cornus and sparkling crystals together with the weight of the Cymbidium orchids sway gently as the bride walks across the sand...

JAMAICA

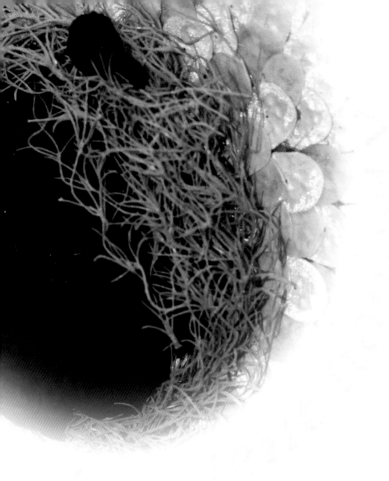

Who wouldn't want to create impact on their big day by carrying this fabulous bridal bouquet? Hundreds of transluscent Lunaria annua (Honesty) discs have been glued on to a fibreglass plate, whilst a bouquet of the richest red 'Grand Prix' roses are placed through the centre. Tillandsia contrasts against the opulence of the plate and the rich velvety texture of the roses. Rose petals continue the colours right down the design...

lamb

pure & simple

pure and stunningly simple in form - a Carmen rose with an innovative twist. Petals of contrasting Jacaranda roses are intermingled with those of the rich red roses. A pearl distinguishes the cenre, and several Aralia and variegated hedera leaves frame the bouquet. Perfect for detailed gowns...

A BRIDAL RIBBON

a romantic, twenty first century alternative to the more traditional bridal bouquet and which should be carried through a loop over the arm, allowing it to flow gracefully behind you. The floral ribbon is constructed of a melee of natural elements includ ing Dendrobium orchids, rosebuds, Lunaria annua discs, panicum grass, Marabou feathers, Gre villea robusta leaves, pre served Hydrangea florets, skeletonized leaves, sisal, hundreds of pearls and tiny heart shaped beads. A sensual creation for the romantic at heart.

claire

♥ 29

CLASSIC OPULENCE

suited to a sophisticated bridal gown this bouquet uses choice materials in a structured way, and oozes style, sophistication and class. The stems of the beautiful Zantedeschia are used as a feature, by binding them tightly with gold bullion wire.   A cluster of Camellia x williamsii 'Hope" take centre stage, surrounded by Viburnum opulus 'Roseum' and Viburnum tinus. Romantic, structured, and very special...

coral carter

♥ 31

DIAMONDS

orchids

are a

girls best friend

whilst diamonds may be said to be a girl's best friend when a bouquet

is added it must have double the appeal! This fairytale bouquet made

from Dendrobium orchids, 'Avalanche' roses and Gypsophila 'Million

Stars' creates the bouquet which is further enhanced by dozens of

glass diamante beads that dance in the light as the bride walks to

meet her groom... The Steel grass handle creates a dramatic carrying

feature.

karen

heavenly apricot

34

a dreamy bridal
bouquet full of
movement and
style... Beautiful
Mango' Zantedeschia
form the
outline of the
bouquet along
with some curvaceous
stems of Salix
tortuosa that are
just showing
their new spring
growth. Leucadendron
'Pincushion'
add strength
and texture to
the design, whilst
a cluster of 'Renate'
roses emphasises
the focal area.
A graceful creation
made with romance
uppermost in the mind

MINIMILIST CHIC

a tactile, bouquet, packed full of textures and colour. Designed for a thoroughly modern bride wearing a straight, elegant gown and wishing to steer away from conventional styles.

A single stem of downy Heliconia rostrata contrasts beautifully with the colourings and textures of the Anthurium 'Pistache,' Zantedeschia 'Aurora' and Skimmia. Simple in style, high in 'wow' factor...

the carmen rose

A romantic, sensual bouquet in a soft yet rich colour theme... the classic Carmen rose is fashioned from many individual Vendella roses, and is just perfect for the modern bride requiring a bouquet that oozes simplicity, style and panache. The bouquet is surrounded by a vine collar which is decorated with sisal, beads and silken cord.

purity

margaret stewart

fragrant Jaminum officiale cascades

gently down from this gracious hand-tied

bouquet of Phalaenopsis orchids, and

'Akito' roses enclosed in a bear grass

collar. Perfect for a low-key ceremony

where style and simplicity is top priority.

margaret s

stewar

the orb of love

as the happy couple begin their lifelong journey together discovering the secrets of the world, a bridal bouquet that features a sphere covered in ivy leaves and wrapped with gold bullion wire becomes the central point from which the whole of the design radiates - and sums up perfectly the significance of the occasion. The cage of Salix is surrounded by Blush Zantedeshia, with lime green Cymbidium orchids massed at the tying point thereby creating a second focal area. Perfect for the bride who craves something that little bit different...

mystique

a bouquet full of mysticism and atmosphere... the heavy gauge wire glitter ball begins the design and creates the foundation for the bouquet. A change of atmosphere is achieved with the simple carnation sphere hidden within, floating and free moving. The lilac freesia, Dendrobium orchids and threaded beads cascade over and around the two orbs creating an aura of mystery and movement for a magical occasion...

L O V E   I S   I N   T H E   A I R

soft, sensuous colourings for a romantic wedding day hand-tied bouquet. This bouquet has been designed to be held to the side of the body as an upright bouquet, it is also able to double up as an arrangement for the reception. Three apricot Zantedeschia give height, which is strengthened by a stiff column of Buxus. Around the base, materials are tightly packed - 'Leandra' roses, 'Princess Irene' tulips, Bouvardia and 'City of Bradford' hyacinth. The shape is emphasised with a collar of foliage which includes Coral fern, Myrica gale and Aralia leaves.

a touch of the luxurious in this bouquet of style and sophistication. The cushion base is made of dozens of transclucent discs of Lunaria annua, the cascading flowers on top provide a total contrast to the shimmering base. Brightly coloured Vriesea 'Tiffany' stunning Phalaenopsis orchids and Dischidiab pectenoides are complemented by ivy berries, and delicate trailing foliage. A bouquet of contrasts, delicate and strong, pastel and vibrant...

coral carter

sensuality

an upright bouquet designed to tantalise the senses with an exciting array
of flowers and foliage in sharp clear colours. High on style, the bouquet
is designed to move gracefully as the bride carries it. A single stunning
Anthurium bloom nestles tightly into the focal area, surrounded by Tulip
'Lindberg,' whilst Zantedeschia 'Aurora' cascade downwards. Further
contrasting textures are included in the form of Phalaenopsis orchids, the
soft feathery Tillandsia and seductive, trailing Jasminum.

inspiration
from
the garden...

a plant and garden lover's bouquet, brimming full of over twenty different types of flower and foliage, in a striking combination of colour. This flowing bouquet is to be held to the side of the body, where the full beauty of the design may be seen at it's best. Flowers included are the seductively fragrant 'Jacaranda' rose and Hellebores which form the focal area. Foliage include the beautiful near black Opiopogon planiscapus 'Nigrescens,' Columnea domestica, Chlorophytum and Rosemarinus officiale.

inspiration
from
the garden...

metamorphosis

...imagine, an open space filled with natural light and pale hardwood floors. This structure on a wrought iron stand evolves from a fibreglass bowl covered with layer upon layer of natural plant material, which strengthens the form and structure within each layer. The addition of Crocus bulbs, stems of Eucharis and pure white Hyacinth completes the metamorphosis of the structure.

NATURE'S HARVEST

each season holds it's own mysterious charm, long sultry summer days give way to the shorter days of autumn, and welcoming, cosy evenings around an open fire... this contemporary tree in geometric style made of preserved moss, Cornus, skeletonized leaves, dried pumpkin seeds and Eucalyptus robusta pods remind us of the passing seasons and the beauty to be had in nature's most simple materials. The seed... the beginning of all life...

secrets within...

flowers are often capable of expressing sentiments that words cannot... the pure white 'Akito' roses, Grevillea 'Spider Man,' 'Prado' carnations and Trachelium nestle closely within a framework of Muehlenbeckia and wired twigs. This framework quietly extends over the flowers giving a three dimensional effect and the ability to observe the flowers hidden within...

Kind hearts are the garden

Kind thoughts are the roots

Kind words are the blossoms

Kind deeds are the fruits.

Anon

au natural

the delicate balance between man and
nature is fragile indeed... this gentle,
ethereal arrangement demonstrates
that fragility and evokes a feeling of
calm and peacefulness - a framework of
willow encloses some bold stems of
majestic Frittilaria, along with stunning
deep purple Zantedeschia, grasses and
foliage. Dried Aspidistra and Phormium
give strength to the design. Duck weed
floats on the clear glass dish...

togetherness

an aura of peace, tranquility and togetherness is symbolised in this stone pool arrangement. Pairs of Zantedeschia 'Best Gold,' and French tulip 'Maureen' take the leading role, whilst a cluster of Ranunculus sits close to the water, where their reflection creates yet another dimension. The clean stems of the Callas contrast strikingly with the rough ivy root and the rough hewn stone container...

a arrangement of solace and quiet...

rebirth from desolation

an abstract arrangement originating
from thick stems of cacti onto which
spheres of Indian moss and lengths
of Corylus have been attached as a
framework into which the flowers
are worked.   Dramatic Monstera
deliciosa leaves, Aralia, Galax and
Pandemues add to the shape and
create movement.   An autumnal
selection of Anthurium, Oncidium
orchids, 'Alexis' roses and Gloriosa
complete the dramatic effect of the
design.

stylish gloriosa

a hand tied construction that oozes
style and sophistication. A modern
design in a striking combination of
colours that uses modern techniques
to maximum impact. Materials include
'Black Baccara' roses, Viburnum
opulus 'Roseum, Gerbera and the
fabulous Gloriosa..

Nature's Own

From it's origination in a ceramic bowl, this design looks as if it has always been there... growing from around a mound of bark, mosses and stones. The plants and flowers are arranged with nature in mind, allowing them to follow their own line. The Anthurium spathes are placed high whilst the delicate orchids are protected within as nature intended.

"Nature is a place where you can relax, go into another world, find yourself, and yet get lost within it's beauty..."

PENTHOUSE STYLE

where city chic meets country casual. Arranged for a low occasional table in a smart minimilist pent house suite, the arrangement in a low bowl features moss close to the base - giving it's country feel. From that simple base style erupts stark white Anthurium, Zantedeschia and Longiflorum lilies. A single Monstera deliciosa leaf creates an area of shade...

vinny yeates

as nature all around us reawakens from the long winter months, fresh green buds emerge from brightly coloured Salix, and spring hyacinth bulbs throw forth their majestic blooms, delicate Muscari pushes its way through the moss. Pure white Eucharis look down gracefully on the scene... all's well with the world.

ROUGH TERRAIN

vibrant colours are the dominant feature in this arrangement full of contrasts and textures. A beautiful glass container is made even more interesting by filling with stems of Salix and retaining the transparency of the vase. The arrangement itself is jam-packed with textures and colours making a total contrast to the transparent base. Leycesteria stems are cut at a sharp angle against which are groups of 'Black Baccara' roses, Helianthus, Viburnum opulus 'Roseum' and Grevillea 'Spider Man.'

meandering
mangoes
meandering
mangoes
meandering
mangoes
meandering
mangoes

an intriguing design full of movement and 'wow' factor using the beautiful and stylish 'Mango' Zantedeschia together with tulips that are entwined within the focal area on a moss covered foam sphere. The arrangement rests comfortably on a clear glass vase filled with 'make believe' ice, to give another dimension to the overall concept...

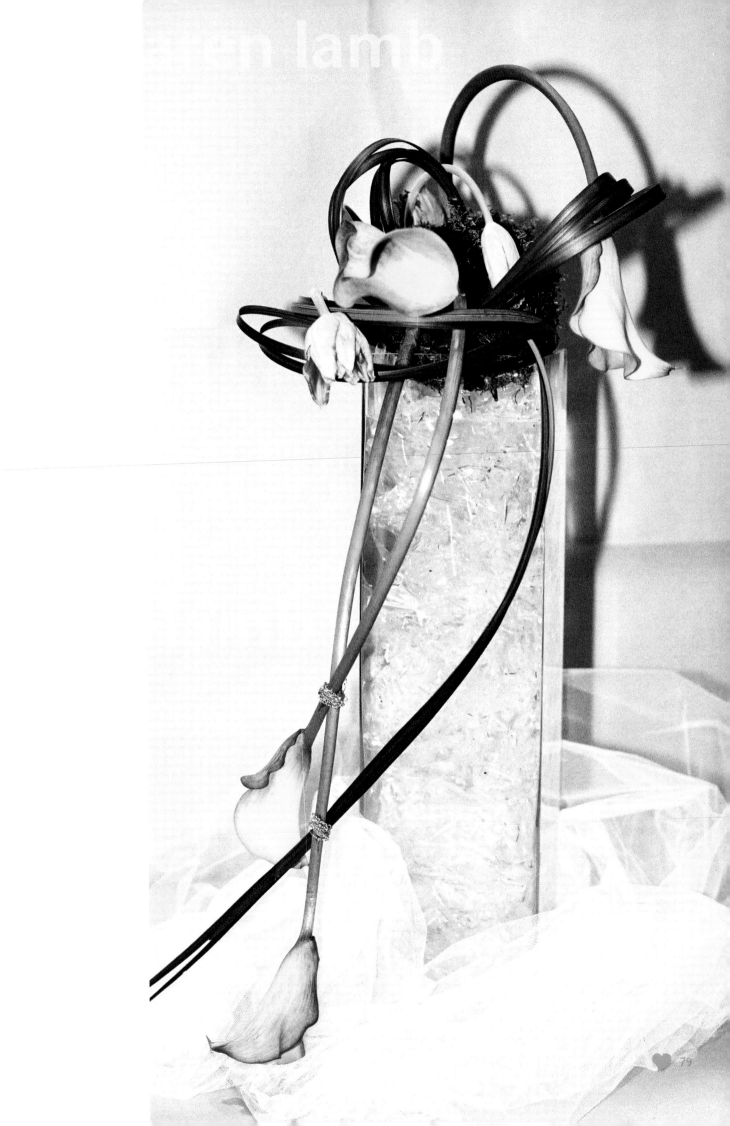

REFLECTIONS

REFLECTIONS

an arrangement of contrasts. Shallow pools filled with water, hewn out of a rugged piece of rock, provide areas of quiet and tranquility. Materials of different form and texture arranged in groups soften the hard stone. Colour is important... time stands still...

reaching

for the stars... this

light,   ethereal

arrangement   has

almost fairytale quali-

ties with it's towering

Eremeurus   spires,

cascading vines and

exquisitely   detailed

areas   that   shelter

under fine Coral fern

umbrellas.   Areas of

peace and tranquility

in amongst the bustle,

wide open spaces to

allow   the   mind   to

wander, strong and

fragile forms emulat-

ing   our   innermost

feelings,   happy

vibrant   colours   to

make the heart glad...

s
k
y
s
c
r
a
p
e
r

a living painting of sculptural form. Vibrant tropical flowers give movement to the quiet and understated mossed base that acts as the canvas. Musa (banana flower) links the flower material to the stand, whilst Phalaenopsis orchids in vibrant colours trail elegantly through the design. Anthurium, Allium and Zantedeshia add more splashes of dramatic colour whilst Monstera deliciosa and Phormium tenax leaves intensify the sculptural form...

It is not the language of the painters but the language of nature to which one has to listen...

Van Gogh

ABSTRACT ART

retro chic

encapsulated in a clear glass cylinder, this retro candy coloured arrangement makes a dramatic fashion statement. Straight sticks form the outline shape, whilst a limited number of individual stems of choice materials add the interest. A couple of Ornithogalum arabicum bring the eye upwards, and made visibly aware of their beautiful lime green stems.

imagine a misty morning in high summer when the anticipation of a perfect day fills the air... The mist of early morning creating an ambiance and atmosphere all of it's own - the scent and colour of summer flowers heightening the senses. Lilac sweet peas, vibrant orange Sandersonia, soft cream Zantedeschia and vanilla Germini intertwined with Clematis vine, Typha grass and sisal.. Sensuous, calming and memorable

contemporary chic

an arrangement in contemporary style that shows strength and fragility... the solid base container is packed with many stems of Birch. In stark contrast papery petalled poppies, velvety iris, vibrant roses and classic Zantedeschia peep above the solid form created by the twigs. Lengths of stripped Smilax overlay the design providing another contrast in colour, texture and form.   Nature's diversity shown in extreme...

the old rugged cross, emotive words for many people..
this rustic wooden cross made of Salix, ivy and various
branches bound together with supple bands of Betula,
makes a strong statement. Pure white Zantedeschia
add dramatic movement to the otherwise rigid form of
the cross. Stoical, immortal.

IN MEMORIUM

dusky succulents

a beautiful tribute that's both traditional and of the moment... the time honoured ring shape echoing the sentiments of never ending affection, which together with modern weaving techniques makes this a tribute to be remembered for a long while. The strong form of the Phormium tenax leaves woven around the frame, create pockets for groups of Eustoma russellianum 'Mariachi Green,' Aeonium and Echeveria. The soft, dusky texture of the succulents contrasts perfectly with the fragile, papery petals of Eustoma, and the strong Hedera and Aspidistra elatior.

emotion

designed for a woodland burial, the sentiments and feelings of the moment are depicted in the tumbling and entwining flower and plant material. Based upon a framework and with mossed tubes to provide a water source, each of the flowers is given it's own space. The Zantedeschia are left free and embellished with gold and silver finials - showing care and heartfelt attention to detail...

fabulous soft creams, ivories and greens are the subtle shades used within this design to represent sympathy, within this stunning fibreglass container. The globe's lid enables materials to be woven through the cracked structure. 'Aremis' roses, Lilium longiflorum, tulips and Viburnum opulus 'Roseum' are carefully arranged with stems of Lily grass, and Asparagus sprengerii adding to the detail.

GLOBAL SYMPATHY

for a lost love...

an unashamedly romantic tribute to a lost love... eternal love signified by the wreath - the shape that has no beginning nor end and using flowers that have special personal significance. Papery and ethereal Ranunculus, dark purple Helleborus, parrot tulips, Bellis, pure white Muscari, tiny rosebuds and lots of garden foliage - Taxus, Viburnum tinus, ivy and Escallonia to name but a few. Clematis vine, just bursting into flower is strewn over the flowers along with fine stems of bear grass.   Until the end of time...

We need time to dream,
time to remember,
and time to reach the infinite.
Time to be.

Gladys Taber

this evocative tribute is a parting gift of never ending love. Red Cornus and ivy is woven around the base, into which groups of choice and meaningful flowers have been carefully positioned. Deep pink Phalaenopsis orchids, rich, ruby red 'Delilah' carnations, fragrant 'Jacaranda' roses, Zantedeschia and hellebore nestle snugly within the framework. A tribute brimming with love and attention to detail...

last love

an abstract interpretation of the traditional cross tribute. Perfectly tailored, and full of emotion and feeling. The strong form of the cross fashioned from fine stems of Cornus is softened and enhanced by the flowing flower material, beautiful Gloriosa, long slender Zantedeschia 'Aurora' and Tillandsia. A flourish of Anthurium 'Amigo' and a group of Tulip 'Lindburg' create a stunning focal area from which all the flowing materials radiate...

CALLUNA
A HIGHLAND TRIBUTE

traditional Scottish heather, grouped as a feature in this dramatic cross tribute, along with stunning Zantedeschia, arranged in an abstract way on a formal base of ivy leaves softened with delicate trails of Jasminum officiale. Masculine and emotive..

for a woodland burial

flowing from a container made from resin and resembling roughly hewn wood, the flowers in this design hold many memories of special moments experienced throughout a lifetime. The wood-like container hints at strength of character and steadfastness. A melee of flower material in a riot of colours gives a happy, relaxed touch to the tribute, for what may be an otherwise sombre day... Materials used include Hedera erectica, Zantede-schia, 'Madeleine' roses, clematis vine and Pittosporum.

"The amen of Nature is always a flower." Oliver Wendell Holmes

for eternity

this tribute emphasises the poignancy experienced during life's long journey. The flower blanket has layers of meandering natural materials that signifies the ever changing times in which we live, and as a reflection of our experiences. The weaving of life's rich tapestry is complex, the tribute is simple, yet detailed, modest and intricate, the colours are soft whilst at the same time dramatic, utilising materials of both simple and sculptured form... clear clean forms include Sandersonia, French tulips, Zantedeschia 'Mango.'

a noble tribute for the celebration of life...

never
ending
love

symbolising never ending love, the wreath
has been a popular tribute for centuries...
this somewhat avant garde interpretation
made from fine stems of Cornus and rose
brier, is decorated simply with a pair of
Zantedeschia 'Aurora,' Tulip 'Lindberg,' ivy
root and Hydrangea. A couple of strikingly
beautiful Anthurium 'Amigo' form the focal
point of the design. The rich vibrant colour
scheme reaffirms the feeling of never
ending love...

a token of love

rich ruby red carnations, stunning Gerbera and vibrant Celosia argentea form the base of this colourful wreath with a hint of the exotic. A flourish of Anthurium create a feeling of opulence and luxury... to say "our thoughts are with you..."

springtime sympathy
springtime sympathy

a thoughtful and beautiful arrangement of spring flowers and foliage that speaks volumes and conveys a heartfelt and sincere message of sympathy. Jostling together in a rustic fibreglass bowl a vibrant selection of flowers are arranged within a wire framework. Eryngium, tulips, Limonium, Muscari and Viburnum opulus 'Roseum' peep out from the meandering lily grass

SPRING SUNSHINE

'I wandered lonely as a cloud' - begins the famous poem by William Wordsworth. 'When all at once I saw a crowd, a host of golden daffodils...' This tribute uses the glorious daffodil for a traditional tribute with a modern twist. The basing has been carried out by splitting the daffodils which gives a rippled effect. A meandering path of moss and gnarled branches leads to the cluster of 'Tete a tete' narcissus...

coral carter

'til the end of time

taking inspiration and feeling from the wonderful pireri bowl, this sympathy design, hints at eternity. The form, texture and thickness of the ancient wood hints at strength and continuity, whilst the flowers themselves are far more fleeting. Beautiful Gloriosa, Dendrobium orchids, Zantedeschia and French' Avingnon' tulips create dramatic lines of colour throughout the design, to lift the spirits and soothe the soul...

A GARDENER'S DREAM

a sympathy basket packed full of every gardener's treasures, reminders of many happy hours spent nurturing and tending seedlings, plants and shrubs. Evocative too, of far distant shores, with the inclusion of some exotic species, Anthuriums form a gracious outline to the design, whilst almost black Zantedeschia cascade overhead. Hellebores, Hypoestes, pansies, roses, dahlia, Camellia and Selaginella, mingle happily with mosses and a medley of garden and tropical foliage...

a
classic
sentiment

this timeless design of a wreath - signifying the full circle of life - is given a fresh and contemporary look. The simple Buxus (Box) ring has been draped with a floral ribbon of Dendrobium orchids, Chrysanthemum santini 'Kermit' foliage and sticks bound onto bullion. It shows both simplicity and complexity together with the tenderness of emotion...

vinny

CONTRASTS

sometimes, just sometimes, when the inevitable happens - the contrasts feel so enormous. The loss, the finality, the dark moods contrasting with serenity, peace and hope. The sphere represents the world changing forever, whilst the bound black sticks represent the inconsolable mood. The two pure white stems of Zantedeschia meandering across the design give out a message of purity and hope.

FLORISTRY

CORAL CARTER NDSF AIFD FSF   Coral Carter NDSF & Anne, 11 Market Place, LONGRIDGE, Preston PR3 3RS Tel:01772 783617

CLAIRE COWLING ICSF MSF Orchard House, CONEY WESTON, Bury St Edmunds, Suffolk IP31 1HG Tel/fax:01359 221421

KAREN LAMB NDSF AIFD CAFA FSF, Flowers by Karen, 1-3 Oxford Street, GUISLEY, Leeds, West Yorks LS 20 9AX Tel: 01943 873492 www.flowersbykaren.com www.flowers-delivered.co.uk

MIKE SHAPCOTT Fleurette of Lymington, 26a The Roundhouse, St Thomas Street, LYMINGTON, Hants SO41 9NE Tel: 01590 674828

NINA SHERSON NZPFA NDSF AIFD FSF, Earthworks International, 23 Marylebone High Street, LONDON W1 Tel: 0171 2246283

MARGARET STEWART NDSF FSF 395 Clarkston Road, GLASGOW G44 3JN Tel: 0141 6378466

NEIL WHITTAKER NDSF AIFD FSF Design Element flowers with passion & style, 67 Liverpool Road, IRLAM, Manchester M44 6EH Tel: 0161 7757039 www.thedesignelement.co.uk

JIM WILLIAMSON Wm Williamson, Beechwood Nurseries, UPHALL, EH52 6PA
Tel: 01506 811433 www.myflorist.co.uk
VINNY YEATES Flowers by Lucy, 53 High Street, KILKENNY, Eire

PHOTOGRAPHY

for CORAL CARTER NDSF AIFD FSF, John Horby, 36A Derby Road, LONGRIDGE, Preston PR3 3JT Tel: 01772 783391

for CLAIRE COWLING ICSF MSF, NINA SHERSON NZPFA,AIFD, NDSF, FSF & MIKE SHAPCOTT, Peter Griffin, GGS Photo Graphics, 1 White Lodge Business Park, NORWICH, NR4 6DG
Tel: 01603 622500

for KAREN LAMB NDSF, AIFD, CAFA, FSF, ANDREA BARRETT, Lincroft House, Landseer Drive, BRAMLEY, Leeds, LS13 2QU

for MARGARET STEWART NDSF FSF & JIM WILLIAMSON NDSF FSF, STUDIO CEE, 35 Elderpark Workspace, 100 Elderpark Street, GLASGOW G51 3TR Tel: 0141 445 5200

for NEIL WHITTAKER NDSF AIFD FSF Don Sinclair LBIPP LMPA, The Parr Lane Studio, 355 Parr Lane UNSWORTH, Bury Lancs BL9 8PJ Tel 0161 766 3844 www.parrlanestudio.co.uk

for VINNY YEATES AIFD Seamus Costello

ACKNOWLEDGEMENTS

I seem to have this kind of 'knack' of having little gems of ideas, without any kind of regard for the feasibility of the actual time scale involved. This project has been no exception... only a short while ago, I discussed the idea behind this book with some very respected colleagues within the floristry industry - colleagues who have a far wider knowledge than my own - to see what they thought about it. It was important to me that these people would give honest opinions, not only to the feasibility of the project, but also whom to approach. I have not been disappointed. The nine florists who have contributed have all come up with beautiful designs in a very short while. To you all 'a huge bouquet of thank you's.' As always, with these kind of projects, the floristry is only the beginning. Thank you to all the photographers involved, who have contributed much to the overall effect of the pieces. It is with great pride and pleasure that I thank Ben Cowling for a grand job well done and Colin Barber for collating everything ready for the printers. A big thank you to Jane Lambert for proof reading. Thanks also to all at Reflex Litho for ensuring that this, the finished article, is what we had hoped for. Finally, I would like to give my thanks to all at home who always seem to take mother's little ideas in their stride. For the weeks when this was being brought together from that seed of an idea, to this, the fruits of our labours - they have been patient and understanding. We hope that you too have enjoyed all the pieces that we have enjoyed creating, and that you have gained some inspiration from the designs, in our celebration of the 'Best of British...'

INDEX